HABITS MATTER

HABITS FOR PERFECT LIFE

PARTHASARATHY G

Made with ♥ on the Notion Press Platform
www.notionpress.com

Dedicated to friends and family...

Contents

Contents

Prologue

Everyone living in the world has different habits and that is one of the important elements that make up their life. Repeating any action often is called habit.

Doing something over and over becomes easy and familiar. The more we repeat a habit, the easier and more permanent it becomes. This is the power of habit.

To live a happier, more fulfilling life, some changes in your regular habits are necessary. Habits can be good or bad. It is important to develop good habits and avoid bad ones. Good habits help you succeed in life.

In this book you will learn about some good and noble habits that will elevate you to greater place.

ONE

MAKE THE MORNING AN EXCITING ONE

If we take a closer look at our days, we can see one thing. That is, we realize that our morning and mood sets our tone for the rest of the day. A good energizing morning is a weapon that leaves you energized, and armed to face the world. So, make it a habit to cheer yourself up every morning.

How to develop this habit:

Do any of the following in the morning as per your schedule.

Meditate, do yoga, exercise, list everything you want to do in your life or for that day in particular, watch a good inspirational video or listen to your favorite song before leaving the house.

There are many ways to help one have more energy in the morning. While the above tips help many people in the short term, it's important to create long-term habits that will help them feel energized throughout the day.

A person can regularly practice a combination of having good sleep at night and best morning routines to help them gather enough energy in the morning.

Overall, making your morning an exciting one can have many advantages for your productivity, mindset, health, time management, and creativity.

- **Increased productivity:** Starting your day with excitement and enthusiasm can help you get motivated and focused. This can lead to increased productivity throughout the day.
- **Positive mindset:** When you start your day on a positive note, it can help you maintain a positive mindset throughout the day. This can help you handle stress and challenges better and can improve your overall mental health.
- **Improved health:** Excitement and enthusiasm can help boost your energy levels, which can lead to better physical health. Additionally, if your morning excitement involves exercise or healthy habits, this can contribute to better overall health.
- **Better time management:** By making the most of your morning and getting started early, you can set yourself up for a more productive day. This can help you better manage your time and avoid feeling rushed or stressed later in the day.
- **More creativity:** Starting your day with excitement and inspiration can also help boost your creativity. This can be especially helpful if your work involves creativity or problem-solving.

Try to make the morning an exciting one, an opportunity to change yourself for a better day!

ÞÞÞ

TWO

SMILE

We think that when we are happy, we tend to smile. But actually, it is not like that.

We smile because we are happy, and smiling releases certain hormones including dopamine and serotonin. It makes us happy.

Although not entirely convincing, researchers have found that there may be a close link between smiling and happiness, suggesting that facial expressions when we smile may have a moderate effect on emotions.

That doesn't mean walking around with a fake smile on your face all the time. But the next time you feel down, smile and see what happens. Or try starting each morning by smiling at yourself in the mirror.

The habit of smiling can have many benefits, including:

- **Improved mood:** Smiling triggers the release of endorphins, which are natural feel-good chemicals in the brain. This can help improve your mood and make you feel happier.
- **Reduced stress:** Smiling can help reduce stress levels by lowering the heart rate and relaxing the body. This can

help you feel more relaxed and calm.

- **Increased social connection:** Smiling is a universal sign of friendliness and can help you connect with others. It can make you appear more approachable and likeable, which can lead to more social interactions.
- **Improved communication:** Smiling can help you communicate more effectively with others. It can make you appear more confident and relaxed, which can help you express yourself better.
- **Improved health:** Smiling can also have physical health benefits. It can help boost the immune system, lower blood pressure, and reduce pain.

Has anyone ever told you to cheer yourself up and smile? This is not the most welcome advice, especially when you are unwell, tired or out of sorts. But there's a really good way to turn that anger around. That's the smile. Science shows that the act of smiling can lift your mood, reduce stress, boost your immune system, and extend your life. And smiling helps to avoid fatigue. So, keep smiling and banish fatigue and conquer life.

FOUR

ALWAYS TRY TO STAY POSITIVE

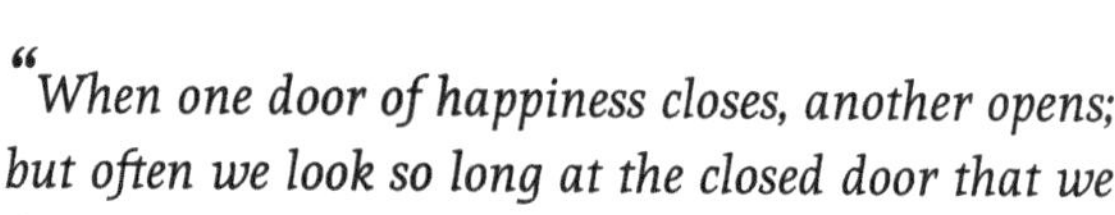

> *"When one door of happiness closes, another opens; but often we look so long at the closed door that we do not see the one which has been opened for us.*
> *- Helen Keller"*

It's okay if something doesn't go well for us, but stay positive and try to make everything better.

Wise and happy people know that bad things happen to everyone. So, when sadness comes, they accept it. They allow themselves the privilege of feeling that desperate or sad emotion fully.

Instead of living in self-pity and complaining about what we can and should have, think about what you can be grateful for and take action.

Focus on the lessons that can be learned from failure, and then work to find solutions to those problems. Face life's challenges with enthusiasm and confidence - and always practice a positive mindset, which will help you to do better in everything you do with effort.

The habit of staying positive can have many benefits, including:

- **Improved mental health:** Staying positive can help improve your mental health by reducing symptoms of anxiety and depression. It can also help you cope better with stress and difficult situations.
- **Improved relationships:** When you are positive, you are more likely to attract positive people and experiences into your life. This can help improve your relationships with others and lead to more fulfilling social interactions.
- **Increased resilience:** Staying positive can help you develop resilience and bounce back from setbacks and challenges more easily. It can also help you stay motivated and focused on your goals.
- **Better physical health:** Staying positive can have physical health benefits, such as improved immune function and lower blood pressure.
- **Improved productivity:** When you have a positive mindset, you are more likely to approach tasks with enthusiasm and energy. This can help improve your productivity and performance.

How to develop this habit:

Accept whatever happens. Do your best to get rid of all pessimism about the situation. Don't let pessimism get you down. It will change your mood and blind your vision towards good thinking.

How do you keep a positive attitude when things don't go your way? Simple: Focus your attention on the good rather than the bad. In psychology, this is referred to as 'cognitive restructuring'.

♡♡♡

FIVE

Do Exercise

"Those who don't make time for exercise will eventually have to make time for illness.

– Robin Sharma"

Exercise is not just for our bodies. Regular exercise can help reduce stress, feelings of anxiety, and symptoms of depression, while exercise can also help increase our self-esteem and happiness.

Exercise improves our mental health, cognitive function and memory, while also reducing our stress and anxiety – all of which contribute to a healthier, happier life.

In fact, research shows that people who exercise for as little as 10-15 minutes a day are happier than those who don't do exercise.

The habit of exercise can have many benefits, including:

- **Improved physical health:** Exercise can help improve cardiovascular health, increase muscle strength and endurance, improve flexibility and balance, and help maintain a healthy weight.

- **Improved mental health:** Exercise can help reduce symptoms of anxiety and depression, improve mood and self-esteem, and reduce stress and tension.
- **Increased energy levels:** Regular exercise can help increase energy levels and reduce fatigue, leading to increased productivity and better quality of life.
- **Better sleep:** Exercise can improve the quality and duration of sleep, leading to better overall health and well-being.
- **Reduced risk of chronic diseases:** Regular exercise can help reduce the risk of chronic diseases such as heart disease, type 2 diabetes, and certain types of cancer.

How to follow this habit:

Do whatever you love to do, be it morning yoga or a favourite sport or a walk in the park. It is better if you exercise as much as you like and according to your time.

SIX

HANG OUT WITH HAPPY PEOPLE

Even happiness is contagious like a disease. When someone smiles at you, you smile back. If someone is rude, you will be rude back. So, hang out only with people whose attitude you want to capture.

This means that if you surround yourself with happy and supportive people, you can easily build confidence, increase your creativity, and generally be happier. Conversely, if you are surrounded by sad and unhappy people, it can be difficult to focus on your own interests and goals. And no matter what you try, they will always say, "It's hard, you can't do it."

The habit of hanging out with happy people can have several benefits, including:

- **Positive mindset:** Being around happy people can help you develop a positive mindset and outlook on life. Happy people tend to have a more optimistic perspective and can inspire you to adopt the same.

- **Reduced stress:** Hanging out with happy people can help reduce stress levels. Positive emotions can help reduce stress hormones in the body, leading to lower levels of stress and anxiety.
- **Increased happiness:** Being around happy people can increase your own happiness levels. Happiness can be contagious, and being around people who radiate positivity and joy can help you feel the same.
- **Improved social connections:** Hanging out with happy people can help improve your social connections. Positive people tend to be more outgoing and approachable, making it easier to build new relationships and strengthen existing ones.
- **Improved overall well-being:** Being around happy people can help improve your overall well-being. Positive emotions have been linked to improved physical health, including lower blood pressure, reduced risk of heart disease, and improved immune function.

Happy people tend to be supportive, kind, and helpful to others. These qualities will also motivate you to be happy. So, surround yourself with positive like-minded people who strive for progress, which will lead you to achieve your dream, goals and reach a higher place in life.

SEVEN

LEARN TO APPRECIATE

In today's fast paced world lifestyle, we forget one thing and that is we fail to appreciate anything.

When you wake up in the morning and when you go to bed at night, remind yourself of the three things you value in life right now. And express appreciation and gratitude in life for them. Having appreciation and gratitude in your life will always help you feel happier. And it also helps to remind you from time to time about important things which you feel missing out in life.

The habit of learning to appreciate can have many benefits, including:

- **Improved relationships**: Expressing appreciation and gratitude can help improve your relationships with others. When you show appreciation, others are more likely to feel valued and respected, leading to stronger and more positive relationships.
- **Improved mental health**: Practicing appreciation can help improve your mental health by reducing symptoms

of anxiety and depression, improving mood, and increasing feelings of happiness and contentment.

- **Increased motivation:** When you appreciate and acknowledge your own accomplishments and the accomplishments of others, it can help increase motivation and drive to achieve more.
- **Improved self-esteem:** Learning to appreciate yourself and others can help improve your self-esteem and confidence. It can help you recognize your own worth and value as well as the worth and value of others.
- **Improved perspective:** Learning to appreciate can help improve your perspective and focus on the positive aspects of your life. It can help you develop a more positive mindset and outlook on life.

Every day, express appreciation and gratitude to your parents and your best friends for being your pillar and bridge. Appreciation breeds happiness. It highlights and evaluates what is important in our lives. And the more you appreciate, the more you will find things to appreciate in your life.

EIGHT

HAVE A GROWTH MINDSET

There are two main attitudes in every human life. One is fixed mindset and the other is growth mindset.

A person with a fixed mindset never changes and never tries to change, believing that their qualities are unchanging. Conversely, those with a growth mindset are capable of change and expansion, and will strive to improve and succeed even when they cannot.

People with a fixed mindset do not handle challenges well and have an ego in everything they do. But people with a happy growth mindset are not like that; They focus on their personal development. They train to achieve their dreams, embrace failure, and look for opportunities to learn something new.

The habit of having a growth mindset can have many benefits, including:

- **Improved learning:** A growth mindset can help improve your ability to learn and adapt to new information and experiences. You are more likely to approach challenges and setbacks as opportunities to learn and grow, rather than as obstacles.

- **Increased resilience:** A growth mindset can help you develop resilience and bounce back from setbacks and failures more easily. You can view setbacks as opportunities to learn and grow, rather than as a reflection of your abilities.
- **Increased motivation:** With a growth mindset, you can approach challenges with enthusiasm and a willingness to learn. This can help increase your motivation and drive to achieve your goals.
- **Improved performance:** When you approach tasks with a growth mindset, you are more likely to put in the effort needed to improve your skills and knowledge. This can help improve your performance and achieve greater success.
- **Improved relationships:** A growth mindset can help you develop a more positive outlook on life, which can help improve your relationships with others. You can view challenges as opportunities to learn and grow together, rather than as sources of conflict.
- **Increased creativity:** With a growth mindset, you are more likely to explore new ideas and take risks. This can lead to increased creativity and innovation.

How to Cultivate This Habit:

Let go of the ego and embrace spiritual love. Look for unity. Seek education, not entertainment. Look for effort. All of these are qualities that foster flourishing, factors that make you happy and success.

Change your fixed mindset to a prosperous growth mindset and you will succeed.

NINE

EAT HEALTHY FOOD

A healthy diet - a great life, a balanced diet - a nutritious life!

The food we eat not only affects our overall physical health but can also bring about a change in our whole mind. A healthy diet gives you the constant energy you need to stay physically active. Hence, healthy eating habits are an important necessity in today's environment.

Eating healthy is about eating the right number of calories knowing how much work you're going to do and how many calories you'll need. So, you balance the energy you consume with the energy you use.

If you eat or drink more than your body needs, the energy you don't use is stored as fat and you gain weight. Eating or drinking less water can lead to weight loss.

You should eat foods rich in carbohydrates and protein to make sure you are getting a balanced diet and getting all the nutrients your body needs. And eating home cooked food is even better. Hobbies like cooking can help you reduce stress. Food hobbies can help improve your mind and physical health.

- Make your diet based on high fiber, starchy carbohydrates.
- More than one-third of your diet should contain starchy carbohydrates. Bread, rice, pasta and cereals are best. Choose high-fiber or whole-grain varieties.
- Eat lots of fruits and vegetables.
- Eat more fish. Fish is a good source of protein and contains many vitamins and minerals.
- Reduce saturated fat and sugar.
- Eat less salt. Eating too much salt can raise your blood pressure. People with high blood pressure are more likely to develop heart disease or stroke.
- To prevent dehydration, you should take plenty of fluids.
- Never skip breakfast. A healthy breakfast that is high in fiber and low in fat, sugar and salt is part of a balanced diet and will help you get the nutrients you need for good health.
- Stay active and maintain a healthy weight. Eating healthy and exercising regularly can reduce your risk of developing serious health problems. It is important for your overall health and well-being.

Remember, developing a habit of eating healthy food is a journey, not a destination. Be kind to yourself and focus on progress, not perfection.

TEN

Learn to Accept

Nothing in life always goes as we plan. We get frustrated when things not happened as per our plan or the unexpected happens. But we never trying to change anything. On the contrary, we are deeply concerned.

Instead, start accepting whatever happens, take lessons or experiences from them and try to change them and you will find relief from unnecessary suffering.

Developing a habit of learning to accept things as they are can lead to a more peaceful and fulfilling life. Here are some tips to help you cultivate this habit:

- **Practice mindfulness:** Mindfulness is the practice of being present in the moment and accepting things as they are. It can help you to become more aware of your thoughts and emotions and reduce resistance to what is happening.
- **Focus on what you can control:** There are some things in life that we cannot control. Instead of dwelling on those things, focus on what you can control. This can help you

to feel more empowered and less helpless.

- **Let go of perfectionism:** Perfectionism can lead to unrealistic expectations and disappointment. Learning to accept imperfection can help you to reduce stress and enjoy life more.
- **Practice gratitude:** Focusing on the good things in life can help you to feel more positive and accepting of what is happening. Take some time each day to reflect on what you are grateful for.
- **Learn from mistakes:** Instead of beating yourself up over mistakes, view them as opportunities to learn and grow. This can help you to be more accepting of your imperfections and mistakes.
- **Seek support:** Accepting difficult situations can be challenging, and it can be helpful to seek support from friends, family, or a therapist. They can offer guidance and help you to process your emotions.

Begin practicing acceptance. Instead of evoking negative emotions, feel the new situation and act accordingly and you will achieve more success.

ELEVEN

SPEND TIME WITH THOSE YOU LOVE

Spending quality time with the people you love is essential to being happy. Even if you are busy, make uninterrupted time for your kids, spouse, family and your friends. That quality time with loved ones will help keep you happy.

We know how difficult it is to schedule family time in today's hectic world. Many families accept a compromise solution and focus on major holidays to spend their time together. But we all know that's not enough, because no one can deny that the joy we spend together and those little moments of quality time help grow our relationship and deepen our bond.

Below is a list of simple, engaging and mindful activities that will help you spend quality time with your family. Some people don't need any effort to keep up with it, but others need some planning. Follow them and inspire your next family activity.

- Have dinner together.
- Take a walk together after dinner.

- Bring your child to school or class.
- Plan a monthly excursion.
- Share family stories.
- Have a heart-to-heart conversation with your teenage son/daughter to know the good aims of today's youth and inspire them.
- Celebrate family traditions.
- Exercise together with your partner.

Developing a habit of spending time with those you love is essential for building strong relationships and fostering a sense of happiness and fulfillment. Here are some tips to help you cultivate this habit:

- **Prioritize time:** Make spending time with loved ones a priority in your schedule. Set aside dedicated time each week to connect with family and friends.
- **Make it a routine:** Incorporate spending time with loved ones into your daily routine. For example, you could have a regular weekly dinner with your family or a standing date with a friend.
- **Be present:** When you're spending time with loved ones, be fully present in the moment. Put away distractions such as phones or laptops and focus on enjoying their company.
- **Plan activities:** Plan activities that you can do together that you both enjoy. This could be anything from going for a hike, to cooking a meal together, to watching a movie.
- **Show appreciation:** Let your loved ones know how much they mean to you. Express your gratitude and appreciation for the time you spend together.

- **Communicate openly:** Healthy relationships are built on open and honest communication. Make an effort to communicate openly with your loved ones, share your feelings and listen to theirs.
- **Be flexible:** Life can be unpredictable, and plans can change. Be flexible and willing to adjust plans to make time for those you love.

TWELVE

LIVE AND ENJOY THE PRESENT MOMENT

The only time one can truly live is the Present Moment. Only at this present moment or time one can have complete control over his life.

We are aware and attentive to what is happening in the moment. So, it is beneficial for everyone to live in the present moment without being distracted by worries about the past or the future.

Staying in a present state of mind is critical to being healthy and happy. It helps you fight anxiety, forget your worries, ground yourself and fully connect with yourself and everything around you.

Although it has become a popular topic in recent years, living in the present isn't just a trendy life tip, it's a way of life backed by science. If you have difficulty focusing on your daily moments, this can have a negative effect on your life. So, you must learn to live more in the present moment.

Developing a habit of living and enjoying the present moment is essential for reducing stress and increasing happiness and fulfillment in life. Here are some tips to help you cultivate this habit:

- **Practice mindfulness:** Mindfulness is the practice of being present in the moment and fully aware of your surroundings. It can help you to focus on the present moment and let go of worries about the future or regrets about the past.
- **Engage your senses:** Engage your senses by noticing the sights, sounds, smells, tastes, and textures of the present moment. This can help you to become more fully present and aware of your surroundings.
- **Let go of judgment:** When you're fully present in the moment, let go of any judgments you may have about the situation or yourself. Simply observe and experience what's happening.
- **Practice gratitude:** Focus on the good things in your life and express gratitude for them. This can help you to feel more positive and appreciative of the present moment.
- **Take a break from technology:** Disconnect from technology and take a break from distractions such as social media or email. This can help you to be more fully present and engaged in the moment.
- **Prioritize self-care:** Take care of yourself by engaging in activities that bring you joy and fulfillment. This can help you to feel more present and alive in the moment.
- **Be spontaneous:** Embrace opportunities for spontaneity and new experiences. This can help you to feel more alive and fully engaged in the present moment.

Stop thinking negatively about your performance and avoid worrying about the future by fully enjoying the present. Minimize moments of depression, focus on new things to improve your memory and make sure to live in the present moment.

THIRTEEN

WORK HARD WITH A PURPOSE

With hard and smart work, you can get incredible results in your life. Everyone knows this. But aimless hard work will only make you feel harder.

Find your purpose in life and then work hard to fulfil that purpose. It will make your life pleasant.

Hard work means putting in extra efforts and extra hours to do some tasks and not giving up until you succeed.

Ultimately, hard work will be the key to your success. A good work ethic creates momentum towards your goals.

Through hard work you can find success, self-growth, confidence building, new opportunities in your life.

Developing a habit of working hard with a purpose can help you achieve your goals and find fulfillment in your work. Here are some tips to help you cultivate this habit:

- **Set clear goals:** Start by setting clear, achievable goals that align with your values and purpose. This will help you stay focused and motivated as you work towards achieving them.

- **Create a plan:** Once you've set your goals, create a plan of action to help you reach them. Break down your goals into smaller, more manageable tasks, and prioritize them based on importance and urgency.
- **Stay organized:** Keep track of your tasks and deadlines by using a planner or scheduling app. This will help you stay on top of your workload and ensure that you're making progress towards your goals.
- **Take breaks:** While it's important to work hard, it's also important to take breaks and recharge your energy. Take short breaks throughout the day to rest and rejuvenate.
- **Embrace challenges:** Don't shy away from challenges or difficult tasks. Embrace them as opportunities for growth and learning, and use them to strengthen your skills and knowledge.
- **Stay focused:** When you're working, stay focused on the task at hand. Avoid distractions such as social media or email, and try to minimize interruptions.
- **Reflect on your progress:** Take time to reflect on your progress towards your goals. Celebrate your successes and identify areas where you can improve.

Hard work with purpose will put you at the top of happiness and success.

FOURTEEN

Listen Actively

Listening is a communication skill. It is the ability to go beyond listening to the words spoken by another person and try to understand the meaning and intent behind them. This habit ensures that we participate enthusiastically in any activity.

Listen carefully and compassionately. Give your full attention to the other person's words. It is a powerful source of happiness as it creates strong bonds between people.

Pay close attention to what the other person is saying or asking first, rather than thinking or writing your own response. Wait until the other person has finished speaking before you respond.

Careful listening is key to understanding. When we are fully engaged in conversations and truly listen, we have the opportunity to clarify confusion. Simply put, do you want your personal and professional relationships to be better? Listen carefully and understand and respond accordingly.

Developing a habit of active listening can help you build stronger relationships, improve communication, and deepen your understanding of others. Here are some tips to help you cultivate this habit:

- **Pay attention:** When someone is speaking, give them your full attention. Avoid distractions such as your phone or other devices, and focus on what the person is saying.
- **Show interest:** Show the speaker that you're interested in what they have to say. Ask questions and engage with them to show that you're actively listening.
- **Avoid interrupting:** Let the speaker finish their thoughts before responding. Avoid interrupting or finishing their sentences for them.
- **Clarify and summarize:** If you're unsure of what the speaker is saying, ask for clarification. Summarize what you've heard to confirm that you understand their message.
- **Use nonverbal cues:** Use nonverbal cues such as nodding or making eye contact to show that you're engaged in the conversation.
- **Avoid judgment:** Avoid making judgments or assumptions about the speaker or their message. Listen with an open mind and try to understand their perspective.

Keep the following in mind when we talk to others.

- Listen fully and listen to what the other person is saying.
- Pay attention to non-verbal cues.
- Maintain good eye contact
- Ask open-ended questions
- Reflect what you hear
- Be patient.

ꝒꝒꝒ

FIFTEEN

ACKNOWLEDGE THE UNHAPPY MOMENTS

A positive attitude is essential in anything. Always remember that good things do not always happen to one person. Bad things happen to everyone. It's a part of life.

If you get bad news or fail, Acknowledge the feeling of unhappiness and allow yourself to feel it for a moment. Then focus on how and what you can do to recover from it.

Remember, no one is happy all the time. So, acknowledge and feel the unhappy moments and focus on what to do next and move forward.

Developing a habit of acknowledging and processing unhappy moments can help you to better cope with negative emotions and experiences.

- **Acknowledge your feelings:** When you're experiencing negative emotions, acknowledge them rather than trying to push them aside or ignore them. Recognize that it's normal to feel unhappy at times.

- **Express yourself:** Find healthy ways to express your emotions, such as through writing, talking to a trusted friend or family member, or engaging in creative activities like painting or music.
- **Practice self-compassion:** Treat yourself with kindness and compassion, especially when you're going through difficult times. Remember that everyone experiences unhappiness at some point, and that it's not a reflection of your worth or value as a person.
- **Practice gratitude:** Focus on the things in your life that you're grateful for, even in the midst of unhappiness. This can help to shift your perspective and improve your mood.
- **Seek support:** Reach out to friends, family, or a professional therapist for support when you're feeling unhappy. It's important to have a strong support system to help you through difficult times.
- **Engage in self-care:** Take care of yourself by engaging in activities that bring you joy and fulfillment. This can help to improve your overall well-being and make it easier to cope with unhappy moments.

SIXTEEN

KEEP A JOURNAL

Writing a diary is a great way to organize your thoughts, analyse your feelings and make any plans.

Anyone can write whatever they want to write and there is no right way to do it. And you don't have to be a literary genius.

And this habit is the one you need the most when you're worried or in a bad mood. You don't have to write every day; you can continue this whenever you feel free. It can be as simple as writing down a few thoughts before you go to bed.

This diary you are writing is not for anyone else. You write it for yourself, and you don't have to worry about whether it's boring, or has perfect grammar, or looks good.

Keeping a journal is a powerful habit that can help you to process your thoughts and emotions, set and achieve goals, and cultivate self-awareness. Here are some tips to help you cultivate this habit:

- **Set aside time:** Schedule a regular time each day to write in your journal. This will help you to make journaling a habit and ensure that you stick with it.

- **Find a quiet space:** Choose a quiet, comfortable space to write in your journal where you won't be interrupted. This can help you to focus and reflect more deeply.
- **Write freely:** Don't worry about grammar, spelling, or punctuation. Write freely and without judgment, letting your thoughts and emotions flow onto the page.
- **Set intentions:** Use your journal to set intentions for your day or week. Write down your goals and plans, and reflect on what you hope to achieve.
- **Reflect on your emotions:** Use your journal to reflect on your emotions and experiences. Write about what you're feeling, and try to identify the underlying causes.
- **Track your progress:** Use your journal to track your progress towards your goals. Write down your accomplishments, and reflect on areas where you can improve.

Don't wait for the perfect day or the perfect experience to write about. Get started today. Many digital mobile apps have also come up for this purpose. So, you don't just have to write on paper, you can also use your favourite mobile apps.

SEVENTEEN

MAKE NEW FRIENDS

Many of us stop making friends after college or marriage age. Making new friends will help you grow as a person, gain new experiences and have a rich social life. So always be blessed to make new good friends.

Even you feel stranger, start a friendly conversation with someone you don't know, and you might just make a new friend. So, that he/she may become your lifelong friend.

Making new friends is a habit that can help you to expand your social circle, build meaningful connections, and enhance your overall well-being. Here are some tips to help you cultivate this habit:

- **Be open and approachable**: Smile, make eye contact, and be open to meeting new people. This can help to signal to others that you're interested in making new friends.
- **Join groups or organizations**: Join groups or organizations that align with your interests and hobbies. This can help you to meet like-minded people

who share your passions.

- **Attend social events:** Attend social events such as parties, community events, or networking events. This can help you to meet new people and expand your social circle.
- **Reach out to acquaintances:** Reach out to people you know, such as acquaintances from work or school, and try to build deeper connections with them.
- **Volunteer:** Volunteering for a cause you care about can help you to meet new people who share your values and passions.
- **Be authentic:** Be yourself and let your true personality shine through. Authenticity can help you to build deeper connections with others.
- **Follow up:** Follow up with people you meet, and make plans to meet up again. This can help to solidify your new friendships.

The consensus is that social relationships make us happier, so make it a habit to always make new friends.

EIGHTEEN

AVOID COMPARING YOURSELF TO OTHERS

Human beings always compare themselves with others. But it is unnecessary or it can be called a disease. When you compare yourself with others you will surely fall. This will leave you feeling more dissatisfied, depressed and anxious with less self-esteem.

Many of us do this unconsciously or without realizing it, but it's important to try to train ourselves to stop. Because, constantly comparing ourselves to others can lead to negative thoughts.

If the comparisons continue, feelings of jealousy, frustration and hopelessness will emerge. If left untreated, chronic anxiety and depression can develop.

Here are some tips to help you cultivate this habit:

- **Focus on your own journey:** Remember that everyone has their own unique journey in life. Instead of comparing yourself to others, focus on your own goals, values, and aspirations.
- **Practice self-compassion:** Be kind and compassionate to yourself, especially when you're feeling inadequate or insecure. Remember that everyone has their own strengths and weaknesses, and that it's okay to make mistakes.
- **Limit social media use:** Social media can be a breeding ground for comparison and feelings of inadequacy. Try to limit your social media use, or unfollow accounts that make you feel bad about yourself.
- **Celebrate your achievements:** Take time to celebrate your own accomplishments and successes, no matter how small they may seem. This can help you to build a greater sense of self-confidence and self-worth.
- **Cultivate gratitude:** Take time each day to reflect on the things in your life that you're grateful for. This can help you to cultivate a greater sense of appreciation for what you have, rather than focusing on what you don't have.
- **Surround yourself with positive influences:** Surround yourself with people who uplift and inspire you, rather than those who bring you down or make you feel inadequate.

Although it's hard to stop comparing yourself to others, but trying to stop can help you find inner peace and happiness.

NINETEEN

CONFRONT STRESS HEAD-ON

Stress is a part of everyone's life and is unavoidable.

But there is no need to be stressed all the time. Stress is not always harmful, sometimes it can even change our attitude towards stress. Sometimes, stress can teach a good lesson.

When you're experiencing stress that you can't handle, remember one thing that everyone has stress. At the same time the soon you face it, and figure out how to deal with it and find an answer. So, you'll realize how much stronger you are than you think.

Here are some tips to help you cultivate this habit:

- **Recognize your stress triggers:** Identify the things that trigger stress for you, such as work deadlines, family obligations, or financial worries.
- **Practice self-care:** Make time for self-care activities that help you to relax and recharge, such as exercise, meditation, or spending time in nature.

- **Practice time management:** Use time management techniques such as prioritizing tasks, breaking large projects into smaller ones, and setting realistic deadlines to help you manage your workload and reduce feelings of overwhelm.
- **Learn to say no:** Don't take on more than you can handle. Be willing to say no to additional obligations that may cause you undue stress.
- **Seek support:** Reach out to friends, family members, or a therapist for support and guidance when you're feeling stressed.
- **Take action:** Take action to address the source of your stress, whether that means having a difficult conversation with a colleague or making a change in your lifestyle.
- **Stay positive:** Practice gratitude and maintain a positive outlook, even during challenging times. This can help you to cultivate resilience and cope more effectively with stress.

TWENTY

DREAM BIG AND TAKE STEPS TO ACHIEVE

We need to dream about our lofty ideals to give life to them. It will drive us forward in life. They excite our minds. And give reasons to live. Dream big and believe that you will achieve it.

Here are some tips to help you cultivate this habit:

- **Set specific goals:** Define your goals in specific and measurable terms, and write them down. This can help you to create a clear plan of action and stay focused on your objectives.
- **Create a plan:** Break down your goals into smaller, more manageable steps, and create a plan of action for achieving them. This can help you to stay motivated and track your progress.
- **Take action:** Take action every day towards achieving your goals, even if it's just a small step. This can help you

to build momentum and make progress over time.

- **Stay accountable:** Share your goals with others and seek accountability from a friend, family member, or coach. This can help you to stay on track and motivated, even when you encounter setbacks.
- **Overcome obstacles:** Expect obstacles and challenges along the way, and be prepared to overcome them. This may require developing new skills, seeking additional support, or changing your approach.
- **Stay flexible:** Be willing to adapt and adjust your plan as needed, based on your progress and feedback. This can help you to stay motivated and avoid burnout.
- **Celebrate your achievements:** Take time to celebrate your successes and milestones along the way. This can help you to stay motivated and reinforce your sense of accomplishment.

Imagine the feelings of how to achieve everything you want and take action. Take a step towards your dream. Take small steps each day to move yourself toward what you want to achieve. Small steps all add up to one day led you to achieve your dream. Devote more time and energy to it.

TWENTY-ONE

MEDITATION

We have heard many people saying that we should meditate to make our life better. Why it's important is that meditation is not just a breathing exercise. It is synonymous with exercise, focus, spirituality and breathing exercises. When you feel everything requires your attention right now, a practice like meditation is much helpful.

This does not mean that we have to learn and follow it completely. Meditation doesn't have to be complicated. The best meditation is to sit quietly with good thoughts in your mind for 5 or 10 minutes. Then slowly you will explore, learn and feel the contents yourself.

Meditation is a habit that can help you to improve your mental and physical well-being, reduce stress and anxiety, and enhance your overall quality of life. Here are some tips to help you cultivate a meditation practice:

- **Find a quiet and comfortable space:** Find a quiet and comfortable space where you can meditate without interruptions.

- **Sit in a comfortable position:** Sit in a comfortable position that allows you to relax and focus your attention. You can sit cross-legged on a cushion, in a chair with your feet flat on the ground, or lie down on your back.
- **Focus on your breath:** Focus your attention on your breath, noticing the sensation of air moving in and out of your body. Allow your thoughts to come and go, without getting caught up in them.
- **Set a timer:** Set a timer for a specific amount of time, such as 5, 10, or 20 minutes. This can help you to stay focused and committed to your practice.
- **Practice regularly:** Set aside time each day to practice meditation, even if it's just a few minutes. Consistency is key to developing a meditation practice.
- **Use guided meditations:** Consider using guided meditations or apps to help you stay focused and engaged during your practice.
- **Be patient and kind to yourself:** Meditation can be challenging, especially if you're new to the practice. Be patient and kind to yourself, and recognize that it's normal to experience distractions and challenges along the way.

When we keep in mind that there is no right or wrong way to meditate, then it is easy to make meditation a daily habit.

TWENTY-TWO

PLAN A TRIP

Instead of always running into a hectic schedule, you can reap the benefits in life by realizing that sometimes travel is necessary and planning a trip somewhere.

There are many benefits of taking a trip, whether it's a short weekend getaway or a long-term adventure. Here are some of the main benefits of travel:

- **Broadens your horizons:** Travel exposes you to new cultures, languages, foods, and ways of life, which can broaden your perspective and expand your knowledge and understanding of the world.
- **Relieves stress:** Travel can help to relieve stress and promote relaxation, as it provides an opportunity to escape from daily routines and responsibilities and focus on new experiences and adventures.
- **Enhances creativity:** Travel can also enhance your creativity by exposing you to new sights, sounds, and experiences that can inspire new ideas and perspectives.
- **Boosts confidence:** Travel can boost your confidence and self-esteem by providing opportunities to overcome challenges, try new things, and build new skills.

- **Builds relationships:** Travel provides an opportunity to build and strengthen relationships with friends, family, and even strangers, as you share new experiences and create lasting memories together.
- **Improves mental health:** Travel has been shown to improve mental health, by reducing stress and anxiety, promoting relaxation, and providing opportunities for self-reflection and personal growth.
- **Creates memories:** Finally, travel creates lasting memories that you can cherish for a lifetime, as you look back on the places you've been and the experiences you've had.

You'll discover that taking a much-needed vacation can reap both mental and physical benefits.

TWENTY-THREE

LET IT GO

If we try something for a long time and it is not possible for us, it is better to leave it. Yes, letting go is not always easy, but letting go is good when new and better things can come your way. Although we feel sad when we give up something, it gives us a kind of relief when we think positively that the struggle is over and new ideas and a path of improvement can be opened.

Make it a habit to let go of things that don't help you, such as complaining, comparing yourself to others, negative thinking, and worrying about past mistakes or worries about the future.

There's no shame in changing your plans if something doesn't go our way.

So let go or forget about any goals that no longer bring you success, even if they look good on paper and focus on the next project.

TWENTY-FOUR

LEARN TO FORGIVE

Get into the habit of forgiving people instead of getting angry over small things.

Maybe someone was late, someone was rude or someone forgot to call you back. Its just resentment tied to a person or a situation, so learn to forgive regardless of all of this and without letting other negative emotions out.

Learning to forgive is a powerful habit that can have many benefits for your mental, emotional, and even physical well-being. Here are some of the main benefits of cultivating the habit of forgiveness:

- **Reduces stress and anxiety:** Holding onto grudges and resentment can create a lot of stress and anxiety in your life. Forgiving others (and yourself) can help to reduce these negative feelings and promote a sense of peace and calm.
- **Improves relationships:** Forgiving others can improve your relationships with them, as you let go of negative feelings and create space for positive interactions.

- **Promotes empathy and understanding:** Forgiveness can promote empathy and understanding, as you try to see things from the other person's perspective and let go of judgment.
- **Enhances self-esteem:** Forgiveness can enhance your self-esteem, as you let go of feelings of victimization and take ownership of your life.
- **Boosts mental and emotional resilience:** Forgiveness can also boost your mental and emotional resilience, as you learn to bounce back from setbacks and keep moving forward.
- **Improves physical health:** Holding onto anger and resentment can have negative effects on your physical health, such as increasing blood pressure and lowering immunity. Forgiveness can help to reduce these negative effects and promote overall health and well-being.

Sometimes, forgiving or letting go of grudges is good for all of us.

TWENTY-FIVE

LIVE HAPPILY IN THE REAL WORLD

Keeping our body, mind and soul in balance is essential for a happy life. Even if the state of one of them changes, it will affect our happiness. So do something every day to improve your overall well-being. Know that taking care of yourself is taking care of family, society and the world.

Happiness is not about having everything you want in life, having a problem-free life, or achieving a certain goal or purpose. Instead, it's about enjoying yourself wherever you are and whatever you're doing.

Living happily in the real world is a habit that can have many benefits for your mental and emotional well-being. Here are some of the main benefits of cultivating this habit:

- **Promotes mindfulness:** Living happily in the real world means being present in the moment and appreciating the beauty of life around you. This promotes mindfulness, which has been shown to reduce stress, anxiety, and depression.

- **Enhances gratitude:** When you focus on the good things in your life and appreciate them, you cultivate a sense of gratitude. Gratitude has been linked to improved well-being, optimism, and resilience.
- **Improves relationships:** When you are happy and content in your own life, you are more likely to have positive interactions with others. This can improve your relationships and social connections.
- **Boosts self-esteem:** When you are happy with your life, you are more likely to feel good about yourself and have higher self-esteem. This can lead to improved confidence and resilience.
- **Increases creativity and productivity:** When you are happy and content, you are more likely to have the energy and motivation to pursue your goals and be creative in your endeavors.

The digital world should only be something that makes our lives better, so live the life you deserve to live without forgetting and getting lost in the digital world.

Books By This Author

All books available at **Notionpress, Amazon and Flipkart** platforms.

To buy, Please search by the title in any of the above mentioned platforms.

Available at **Notionpress, Amazon and Flipkart**

- **15 Inspiring Stories about SWAMI VIVEKANANDA**
- **HOW TO IMPROVE KIDS SELF MANAGEMENT SKILLS**
- **Spiritual Thoughts of The Buddha**
- **CHE GUEVARA (Tamil)**
- **Inspiring Thoughts and Quotes of APJ Abdul Kalam (English and தமிழ்)**
- **Habits Matter - Tamil and English**
- **Learn Tamil Alphabets - With English Pronunciation**
- **Tirukural (For All TNPSC Exams) - Tamil**

9 798889 092568

Printed by Libri Plureos GmbH in Hamburg,
Germany